Email Marketing

How To Protect Your Business When Selling By Email

A Quick Legal Guide™

By Mike Young, Esq.

Copyright Notice

This guide is Copyright © 2019 Michael E. Young (the "Author"). All Rights Reserved. Published in the United States of America.

No part of this guide may be reproduced or transmitted in any form or by any means, electronic or mechanical, including photocopying, recording, or by an information storage and retrieval system -- except by a reviewer who may quote brief passages in a review to be printed in a magazine, newspaper, blog, or website -- without permission in writing from the Author. For information, please contact the Author by e-mail at mike@mikeyounglaw.com or by mail at 5960 W. Parker Rd., Suite 278 PMB 421, Plano, Texas 75093 USA.

For more information, please read the *"Disclosures and Disclaimers"* section at the end of this guide.

First Print Edition, March 2019

Published by Internet Attorneys Association LLC (the "Publisher").

Table of Contents

How To Use This Guide	4
Introduction	6
Chapter 1 - Can The Spam	7
Chapter 2 - Important Spam & Privacy Laws	10
Chapter 3 - Affiliate Promotions	15
Chapter 4 - Making Claims	18
Chapter 5 - Other Deceptive Email Practices	24
Chapter 6 - Email Copyrights	30
Chapter 7 - Email Signatures	37
Quick Start Checklist	39
Do You Need Help?	40
About The Author	41
Rate and Review	42
Resources	43
Disclosures And Disclaimers	46

How To Use This Guide

Each Quick Legal Guide™ is designed as a resource to quickly learn the most important things you need to know about one business legal topic.

In the *Introduction* section, we'll provide a brief overview of what you'll want to do to protect yourself when marketing goods or services by email.

In *Chapter 1*, we'll discuss unsolicited commercial emails (spam) laws in general and how to avoid getting sued or criminally prosecuted for spamming.

Chapter 2 identifies specific important spam and privacy laws...and how to avoid breaking them when marketing by email.

We'll explain how to safely do affiliate promotions by email in *Chapter 3*.

Then in *Chapter 4*, we'll cover the do's and don'ts of making money or health claims about products or services in your emails.

Chapter 5 reveals other common deceptive email marketing practices you should avoid.

How copyright law affects what you can do with email marketing is discussed in *Chapter 6*.

After that, we'll show you in *Chapter 7* how to structure your email signatures to limit your liability exposure.

The guide also contains a *Quick Start Checklist* so you know what to do after reading the guide.

Additional material, including a *Resources* section, is located at the back of this guide. These reference materials should be used as-needed but aren't essential to understanding the topic.

Introduction

Here's a brief overview of the actions you'll want to take to protect yourself when email marketing products or services.

First, you'll craft an email signature you use in all of your email marketing to reduce your legal liability exposure.

Second, you'll make sure your emails comply with applicable spam and privacy laws.

Third, you'll check your affiliate promotions to see if there's anything that needs to be fixed.

Fourth, you'll want to fix your broadcast emails and autoresponder sequences to make sure they're not making illegal claims or contain content that constitutes a deceptive marketing practice.

Fifth, you'll verify your email marketing takes full advantage of copyright law to protect your intellectual property rights and prevent infringement claims against you.

Chapter 1 - Can The Spam

To get started, let's define "spam" so we're on the same page when discussing what it is and how spam laws affect your email marketing.

What Is Spam?

Unsolicited commercial email[1] (known as "spam") is illegal. Note there are two elements that make an email spam:

(1) Unsolicited; and

(2) Commercial

Generally, *both* elements must exist for an email message to be spam.

Unsolicited But Not Commercial

If you send someone an email wishing them a happy birthday, that's not spam. It is unsolicited. But it's not commercial unless you're also trying to sell them something in the same email (e.g. offering a birthday discount on their next purchase).

---

[1] Canada uses the broader term "commercial electronic message" to refer to emails, text messages, social media posts, etc.

Solicited *And Commercial*

Similarly, if someone opts into receiving emails from your business containing special offers, if you send them such an offer, that's not spam. It's commercial but it's also solicited because they requested to receive it.

Unsolicited *And* Commercial

You grab a restaurant's business card[2] and use the email address on it to send the owner a message that's designed to sell the restaurant on using your products or services. That's spam because it's both unsolicited and commercial. The owner didn't ask for you to email him. And the email you sent is clearly commercial.

Why It's Important To Not Send Spam

From a legal standpoint, if you spam you risk one or both of the following bad things happening to you:

1. Civil lawsuit; and/or
2. Criminal prosecution

This means you're risking bankruptcy and even imprisonment if you're targeted for spamming.

---

[2] Even if someone hands you their business card, it's not an invitation to spam them at the email address on the card.

Although it's true there are some people who get away with spamming, there are also many who got nailed for it despite mistakenly believing they couldn't be touched. For example, there is an Australian who was put in a U.S. federal prison for spamming even though he had never been to the U.S. before his arrest.

Chapter 2 - Important Spam & Privacy Laws

Because there are so many laws and regulations around the world, it would be impossible to identify, write, and maintain a multi-volume treatise that analyzed all of them.

This section is based on laws that are (a) most important to North American marketers and (b) used as models by other countries for their laws that cover email marketing.

These spam and privacy laws are…

1. U.S. Controlling the Assault of Non-Solicited Pornography And Marketing Act (CAN-SPAM Act)
2. Canada's Anti-Spam Legislation (CASL)
3. European Union's General Data Protection Regulation (GDPR)
4. California's Anti-Spam Law and the California Consumer Privacy Act of 2018[3]

---

[3] At the time this guide was written, California's 2018 privacy law was scheduled for enforcement beginning in 2020.

Some of these laws and their implementing regulations are stricter than others. However, most email lists will have opt-ins from people who reside in the United States, Canada, or the European Union.[4]

This means your email marketing strategy should err on the side of caution. Don't use tactics that *might* be legal in one country but are clearly illegal in another where you have subscribers.

Here are 7 safe email marketing tactics you'll want to use to avoid spam or privacy-related legal problems....

1. **Get Express Consent From Non-Customers.** Get express consent by using verified[5] opt-ins to your lists. Although it *may* reduce conversion rates to require a prospective subscriber to confirm they want to receive marketing emails from you, it essentially eliminates the risk of someone successfully

---

[4] Blocking opt-ins by geographic region is easily circumvented (e.g. using Virtual Private Network (VPN)) so that's not an effective way to avoid a country's spam laws.

[5] Verified opt-in is also sometimes referred to as "double opt-in" or "confirmed opt-in."

subscribing a third party to your list without their consent.

2. **Time Limit Implied Consent By Customers.** A purchase of your product or service is not permission to send commercial emails to a customer in perpetuity. It's reasonably safe to assume implied consent for about a year after a purchase is made (unless the customer tells you stop). After 12 months, get express consent to continue mailing.

3. **Quick Unsubscribes.** If a subscriber requests you unsubscribe them, do so promptly (7 days or less). If the request to unsubscribe is nasty (e.g. personal attacks on you), consider *blocking* the email address from opting into any of your lists in addition to promptly unsubscribing the person.

4. **Copy of Personal Data.** If a subscriber[6] asks for a copy of the personal data you have

---

[6] Verify the subscriber's identity before releasing sensitive information.

collected about the subscriber, give them a copy of the information at no cost.[7]

    a. Common subscriber data collected by autoresponder services include…
        i. Name
        ii. Email address
        iii. Date and time of opt-in
        iv. Location from where opt-in occurred (city, state/province, IP address, etc.)
        v. Page URL where subscriber opted into list
        vi. Dates, times, and subject lines of broadcast and sequence emails sent to subscriber
    b. If the subscriber is also a customer, you may also have additional personal data, including products or services purchased, shipping address,

---

[7] If there are repeated requests for the same information by a subscriber after you've provided the information, you may charge a nominal fee if you honor the subsequent requests. If you reject subsequent requests, provide a prompt response explaining why (e.g. "We already gave you the information two weeks ago that you're requesting now").

telephone number, etc. Be careful how you supply sensitive data (e.g. last 3 to 4 digits of a credit card or Social Security Number instead of the entire number).

5. **Honor Deletion Requests If Legal To Do So.** If a subscriber requests you delete their personal data, promptly delete the information *unless you're required by law[8] to keep the data.* Delete the personal data in your possession and in third party systems you use (e.g. your autoresponder service, backup data in cloud storage, etc.). Let the subscriber know you've complied with the request or why you can't legally do it.

6. **Stop Marketing When Requested.** Sometimes a subscriber will request you stop using their information to market to them. This means they've withdrawn prior consent, i.e. future commercial emails can be considered unsolicited (spam). Honor the

---

[8] Some governments require certain data be retained for a certain period of time (e.g. insurance and loan applications).

request by unsubscribing them from your list(s).

7. **Port Personal Data Upon Request.** If you collected certain personal data, such as medical history for health insurance lead gen or financial information for a mortgage application, you *might* receive a request to transfer the data to a third party (e.g. a competitor) because your subscriber doesn't want to repeat the process. After verifying the subscriber's identity (to protect sensitive information) you should promptly provide the information in a common electronic format (e.g. CSV, JSON, XML, etc.).

Chapter 3 - Affiliate Promotions

The U.S. Federal Trade Commission (FTC) considers affiliate status to be a "material connection" to the business running the affiliate program.[9]

This means you must disclose your affiliate status when affiliate marketing by email.

Why Disclosure Is Important

In addition to it being the right thing to do from an ethical standpoint, the government wants email recipients to know you're an affiliate before making a decision whether or not to buy what you're promoting.

Because there's a potential for bias when you're being paid as an affiliate. Without knowing your affiliate status, prospects lack an important fact necessary to make an informed purchasing decision.[10]

---

[9] A business that runs an affiliate program is sometimes called an "affiliate program operator."

[10] Other material connections to the affiliate program operator should also be disclosed. For example, disclose if you're related to the program operator, co-own a business together, are cross-promoting to each other's lists, etc.

Sample Disclosure Language

There isn't specific language required for disclosing affiliate status.[11] You can use your own words to disclose this type of a material connection. Here's an example for a product I promote as an affiliate.

> *"Because Scott Haines' 'Shortcut Copywriting Secrets' is such a great course for both new and experienced copywriters, it's one of the few resources I recommend as an affiliate. This means if you <u>get the course through this link</u>, I may be compensated."*

Be sure to use a text font size and color matching the main body of your email message. Don't hide it in small print or in a text color that matches the email's background color so no one can read it. That's not disclosure. It's deceptive.

---

[11] And you don't have to disclose how much you'll get paid as an affiliate either. Just affiliate status.

Chapter 4 - Making Claims About Your Product Or Service

Whether it's your email sales copy, or a testimonial you include in a message, it's important to make sure your money and health-related claims for the products and services you're promoting comply with the law.

What The Wrong Claims Can Cost You

The U.S. Federal Trade Commission (FTC), a state's Attorney General, or another government agency[12] can put you out of business for making the wrong claims. We're talking fines, refunds of the purchase price, triple damages, asset freezes, and restrictions or a ban on future marketing.[13]

And even if you "win" if the government comes after you, the legal fees will likely wipe out any profits generated by making the claims.

---

[12] e.g. U.S. Food & Drug Administration (FDA)

[13] A client rejected an affiliate applicant because he had received two permanent bans by the FTC...one for online marketing and a second for offline marketing. Although the applicant lied on his application, a simple Google search of the applicant's name and FTC revealed the bans.

Of course, there are also consumer protection attorneys who will sue on behalf of your "victims" if there's money to be made. Plus, many consumer protection laws[14] make you pay the other side's attorney's fees and court costs when you lose.

Atypical Results Disclaimers

Some email marketers mistakenly believe they can make earnings or health claims if they include an atypical results disclaimer somewhere in their message.

Example: If you buy *Instant Riches Widget X*, you could earn $12,000 per month like John Smith did. Of course, your results might be different.

Example Testimonial Claim: "I lost 90 lbs. in six months taking Magic Pill X." -Jessica Smith, Hot Springs, Arkansas. Your results may vary but we promise you'll shed weight like Jessica taking just one "magic" pill with your meals.

---

[14] Some email marketers focus on business-to-business (B2B) niches instead of business-to-consumer (B2C) to reduce the risk of getting in trouble under consumer protection laws.

Although these disclaimers *might* help you avoid liability in some states, the FTC doesn't believe such disclaimers are enough.

What Are Typical Results?

Using the second example, let's say you have 10,000 customers buying Magic Pill X. And 40 of them have provided you with testimonials backed by proof (pics, medical records, etc.) showing they averaged 90 lbs. of weight loss over six months while taking the pills.

While these testimonials may be anecdotal evidence the pills work, making a related weight loss claim would be considered deceptive. Why? Because the FTC and some other government agencies assume the other 9,960 customers (who didn't provide testimonials) didn't experience such weight loss...and might have even gained weight.

How To Make Claims The Right Way

Here are two simple solutions:

1. Scientific studies; and
2. Customer case studies backed by evidence

Scientific Studies

Although it's often too expensive to pay for scientific studies to provide you with results you can claim, there may be reputable third-party studies you can rely upon in your email marketing.

Example: You're marketing a business book of the month subscription by email to entrepreneurs. You find a peer-reviewed study in the Harvard Business Review that concludes executives who read one book a month earn an extra $100,000 per year than those who don't read any books.

You *can* cite the study and its findings in your email. However, you *can't* make the claim subscribing to your book service will result in the subscriber achieving similar results. The reader of your email *may* reach that conclusion but you don't have a study showing your subscribers actually earn $100,000 per year.

Example: You market specialty walking shoes to working moms by email. You find a peer-reviewed study in the New England Journal of Medicine that concludes working mothers who walk 30 minutes at lunch time lose an average of 3 pounds monthly and decrease their chance of a heart attack or stroke by 16%.

In your email, you *can* cite the study and its findings. However, you *can't* claim wearing your shoes will cause the purchaser to achieve these results. Let the email recipients make the mental leap by themselves that investing in your shoes results in these types of health benefits.

Customer Case Studies

In your email, you *can* refer and link to legitimate[15] customer case studies to support your claims. Although this guide is not about writing case studies, a good format is to identify (a) the prospect's problem, (b) your product/service as the solution, and (c) the results[16] achieved with your solution.

The case studies you link to should include all of the material facts that led to the results.

---

[15] Never create fake case studies or testimonials. They're deceptive and there's no defense if you get caught.

[16] Don't use stale testimonials or case studies. At least on an annual basis, make sure they're still accurate as far as results. Update or dump them if they're inaccurate.

Example: If a customer who lost 90 lbs. taking your diet pill also worked out three hours a day at the gym and was on a 1200-calorie diet, both the gym workouts and the restrictive calorie diet should be disclosed in the case study as material facts.

And if there's a material connection between you and the customer, that needs to be disclosed too so there's enough transparency for the prospective buyer to make an informed purchasing decision.

Example: If the customer is a company owned by your brother-in-law, you need to disclose the relationship as a material connection.

Keep Good Records

Keep copies of scientific studies and the supporting documentation you have for claims made in case studies. If a government agency contacts you, having these records to back up what you said in your marketing emails reduces the likelihood of a formal government investigation or an expensive lawsuit.

Chapter 5 - Other Common Deceptive Email Practices

In addition to hiding affiliate status (see *Chapter 4*) and making deceptive claims about your product or service (see *Chapter 3*), there are other common deceptive email marketing practices you should avoid.

Some of the most common tactics that cause legal headaches are...

- Exceeding Scope of Permission
- Failing To Disclose Material Connections
- Misrepresenting The Offer
- Using A Fake Sender
- Having A Misleading Subject Line
- Providing A Fake Mailing Address
- Including A Bogus Unsubscribe Link

Exceeding Scope Of Permission

The scope of permission on your opt-in forms is important. Don't go beyond it. Here are examples of deceptive practices where the email marketer goes too far.

Example: The opt-in form says the subscriber will receive weekly emails. However, the marketer sends emails to the list three times a day.

Example: Subscribers opt in to receive a free ebook. The opt-in form says nothing about additional emails. However, in addition to receiving the download link by email, each subscriber gets hit with a 30-day autoresponder sequence of marketing emails.

Example: The opt-in form offers a weight loss checklist and weekly diet tips. However, the email marketer puts the subscriber on a second list without permission that pitches an unrelated "get rich flipping houses" info product.

Failing To Disclose Material Connections

Material connections are key relationships that must be disclosed in your marketing emails so that the recipients can make an informed decision about purchasing the product or service you're promoting.

In Chapter 4 of this guide, we covered the most common material connection - promotion as an affiliate in exchange for a commission.

Yet there are other material connections that are essential facts you should disclose. They include…

- You are related to (or dating) the person whose product or service you're promoting.
- You're promoting someone else's product or service to your list in exchange for them promoting your product or service to their list
- A seminar promoter has agreed to let you speak at his event if you pitch the seminar to your email lists.
- You'll receive a free membership site subscription if you sell X number of memberships to that site.
- You received a free/complimentary/review copy of a product or service in exchange for promoting the product or service (including providing a review).

Misrepresenting The Offer

Don't mislead the email recipient about what's being offered by falsely stating or omitting key facts in your email. Although it's certainly okay to drive email recipients to a sales page to get the details, don't do it deceptively.

For example, let's say you're marketing a product that has a 30-day trial for $7 but its total cost is $297. Claiming in your email that the product only costs $7 misleads the recipient by failing to disclose the $7 is for the 30-day trial.

Using fine print disclosures and disclaimers in your email doesn't help fix a misleading offer either.

For instance, let's say the body of your email offers access to a membership website for $29.95. But the fine print at the bottom of your email discloses the $29.95 isn't the total cost but just the first month's fee. Each month thereafter, subscribers' cards are charged a membership fee of $19.95.

This would be deceptive because email recipients are unlikely to read the fine print disclosing these key terms. The average subscriber would be misled into believing the total cost was $29.95, not a paid monthly subscription.

Using A Fake Sender

To increase open rates, some marketers try to trigger recipient curiosity by using a fake sender name in their emails (e.g. God, Elvis Presley, Yoda, etc.). It's okay to use a pseudonym in your business (e.g. an author's pen name). But impersonating someone famous (real or fictitious) to increase open rates can be deceptive.

Similarly, using a false sender email address to increase open rates (e.g. TaylorSwift@RockStarRich.es) or to prevent reply emails[17] is a deceptive practice.

Having A Misleading Subject Line

A misleading marketing subject line can cause legal issues too. Falsely stating "Your mother has been in a car wreck!," "Your mortgage payment is overdue!," etc. to increase open rates is a deceptive practice.

---

[17] A sender *no-reply@[yourdomainname].com* address isn't deceptive if it's a legitimate email address but merely telling the recipient not to reply to it. Of course, there should be other sender contact methods in the email (e.g. sender address, unsubscribe link, etc.) so the recipient can respond by other means.

Providing A Fake Mailing Address

Don't put a fake business mailing address in your emails to prevent complaints or protect your privacy. If your privacy is a concern, use a valid post office (P.O.) box or a private mailbox (PMB).

Including A Bogus Unsubscribe Link

Make sure your *unsubscribe* hyperlinks work.[18] What's more deceptive than a nonworking *unsubscribe* hyperlink in emails? A bogus "unsubscribe" link that actually subscribes the person to a new list when they click unsubscribe.

---

[18] In addition to being the right thing to do, having a valid *unsubscribe* link makes it easy for you to click and get rid of someone from your list who sends you a nasty reply email.

Chapter 6 - Email Copyrights

In this chapter, we'll cover protecting ownership of your emails using (1) copyright notices and (2) copyright registrations. We'll also discuss fair use of copyrighted emails.

Copyright Notice

To reduce the chance someone pirates your marketing emails and recycles them to their own lists, you'll want to put a copyright notice on your emails below your signature lines at the end of each message.

Example:

Copyright © 2019 <u>Law Office of Michael E. Young PLLC</u>.[19] All rights reserved. Unauthorized duplication prohibited.

This notice is enough to prevent someone from claiming they didn't know about your copyright ownership.

---

[19] Hyperlinking to your website in the copyright notice is optional.

However, the notice is only of limited value unless you also register your copyright.

Copyright Registration

To put some legal teeth behind your copyright, consider copyright registration. In the United States, that's done with the U.S. Copyright Office at the Library of Congress.

You can file online at Copyright.gov. To save money, some email marketers register their emails as a compilation. This means they bundle a group of emails together and register them for a single filing fee instead of separate registrations (and fees) for each.

What's the advantage of copyright registration? It gives you a legal sledge hammer to hit pirates who swipe your marketing emails. Why? Because willful infringers can be liable for up to $150,000 per infringement, attorneys' fees, and court costs.

Fair Use

What the heck is "fair use" and why is it important for email marketing? The concept of "fair use" is the ability to use part of a copyrighted work[20] *without* the permission of the copyright owner under certain circumstances. Unfortunately, fair use is a fact-intensive issue that's resolved on a case-by-case basis.

However, there are guidelines courts use you can also apply to help you decide whether you're dealing with fair use or copyright infringement.

Something New

As a preliminary matter, fair use involves something new, i.e. value-added.[21]

Purpose

Fair use can involve one or one or more of the following purposes: criticism; commentary; parody; reporting news; research; scholarship; and teaching.

---

[20] Whether or not the copyrighted work is registered.

[21] The concept of adding something new that's value-added is sometimes referred to as "transformative."

This means that if you want to use part of someone else's copyrighted work in your emails (e.g. a troll's flaming email sent to you), or someone wants to use parts of your marketing emails without permission, it should be for one or more of these purposes.

Character of Use

Whether the use is commercial (e.g. email marketing) or non-commercial (e.g. non-profit educational) is *a* factor. Commercial use is *less likely* to be considered fair use.

Nature of the Work

Use of a factual work (e.g. excerpt from a news story) is more likely to be considered fair use than use of a fictional work (e.g. a novel).

Quantity and Quality Used

Generally, the *more* you use of a work, the *less* likely it is considered fair use. On the other hand, if you use a small portion of a work that's highly valuable (e.g. the paragraph at the end of a mystery novel that reveals the identity of the killer), that's unlikely to be considered fair use.

Your view of what's the right amount may differ from someone else. For example, the Associated Press (AP) once took the position that fair use was limited to four words from any of its news stories (including the headlines).

Effect on Market

If the use negatively affects the market for the copyrighted work, it's less likely to be considered fair use.

For example, an email that contains excerpts from a book might: (1) reveal so much there's no reason to buy the book; and/or (2) cast the book in a poor light so people are less likely to buy it.

Portraying in a False Light

Caution - Even if use of another's copyrighted work is considered fair use, you can't twist it in your email marketing to portray him in a *false* light that damages his reputation.

For example, don't excerpt a competitor's email out of context to *falsely* portray the competitor as dishonest, unqualified, etc.

What if a troll sends you a flaming email filled with grammatical and typographical errors? To the extent fair use applies to quoting some of the troll's attack in your marketing emails, you still can't *falsely* portray the troll as mentally retarded, functionally illiterate, etc. (no matter how tempting it might be).

When You Can't Rely Upon Fair Use

If you'd like to use someone else's copyrighted work in your marketing emails but fair use doesn't apply, what do you do?

Getting permission (preferably in writing) from the copyright owner is the ideal solution. Sometimes permission is given in advance without asking for it (e.g. an affiliate program operator providing you with template promo emails to use as an affiliate).

However, obtaining permission might not be possible if there's no way to identify the copyright owner or if the material you'd like to use is a troll's email, an anonymous review trashing your product, etc.

In these types of situations, it's important to remember that copyright law doesn't protect ideas, just the way they're expressed.

In your own words,[22] you can describe the idea you're trying to convey. In some cases, it's a hybrid situation, i.e. you take a brief quote (e.g. a phrase or sentence) from the copyrighted work as fair use if it qualifies...and then describe the rest in your own words.

---

[22] Using an article spinner or a thesaurus to simply find-and-replace words isn't enough. That would likely create a derivative work still covered by the original copyright.

Chapter 7 - Email Signatures

If your business structure has a personal liability shield (e.g. a corporation or limited liability company (LLC)), take advantage of that shield by signing your emails correctly.

How do you do this?

The three essential elements of a proper email signature are:

1. Identify yourself by name;
2. List your company title; and
3. Include the full name of your business

Example signature:

Sincerely,

-Roward

Roward Skultz, President
Skarbucks Coffee Corp.

You risk personal liability exposure if you don't make it clear the email is being sent on behalf of your business.

For example, if Howard signed just his name without identifying his title or company name, people could assume he was sending it in his individual capacity instead of for the business.

Quick Start Checklist

Here are five steps you can take to quickly reduce your email marketing legal risks.

- ☒ 1. If your business entity has a personal liability shield (e.g. corporation, LLC, etc.), make sure all of your marketing emails are using the right email signature format. See *Chapter 7*.

- ☒ 2. Stop immediately any of your email marketing (broadcasts or sequences) that is spam. See *Chapters 1 and 2*.

- ☒ 3. Check your affiliate promotional emails to ensure you're disclosing affiliate status to recipients. See *Chapter 3*.

- ☒ 4. Verify you're not making false claims or engaging in other deceptive email marketing practices. See *Chapters 4 and 5*.

☒ 5. If it makes economic sense, register copyrights for your emails. And make sure your emails don't infringe on someone else's copyright. See *Chapter 6.*

Do You Need Help?

Do you have questions about whether your existing email marketing campaigns comply with U.S. law? Or are you looking for other email marketing legal advice?

Let's talk about your legal needs. Go to https://mikeyounglaw.com/appointments/ or call 214-546-4247 to schedule your phone consultation.

Just choose a day and time that's convenient and I'll call you.

Wishing you the best.

-Mike

Michael E. Young, J.D., LL.M.
Attorney & Counselor at Law

About The Author

Since 1994, Internet Lawyer Mike Young has helped business clients prevent and solve legal problems.

President of the Internet Attorneys Association LLC, Mike has a law office in Plano, Texas (a Dallas suburb).

Happily married, he enjoys spending time with his family, walking his dogs, and self-defense training.

To learn more, go to MikeYoungLaw.com. While there, be sure to subscribe to his complimentary newsletter where you will receive important business legal news and tips by email.

Rate and Review

If you have found this guide helpful, please post a positive customer review for it at Amazon.com.

Whether you liked the guide or not, please send me a copy of the review you submitted to Amazon because feedback is important for updates and writing new guides too.

Just email a copy to me at mike@mikeyounglaw.com and I promise to respond.

Thank you.

-Mike

Resources

Caution - just as technology changes quickly, so does the quality of service providers. What's a good resource today may become a poor or obsolete one tomorrow. In short, perform your own due diligence before using any of the following resources. Also note that each of these resources are listed in alphabetical order by topic, not by preference of the Author or Publisher of this guide.

Autoresponder Services

- Active Campaign https://www.activecampaign.com/
- AWeber (affiliate link for service my law firm uses) https://internetlawyer.aweber.com/
- MailChimp https://mailchimp.com/

Copyright Registration

- Canada - http://www.ic.gc.ca/eic/site/cipointernet-internetopic.nsf/eng/h_wr00003.html
- United States - https://copyright.gov/

Email Marketing Experts
- Ben Settle - https://bensettle.com/
- Big Jason Henderson - http://www.BEMInsiders.com

Spam/Privacy Laws & Regulations

- U.S. CAN-SPAM Act of 2003, 15 U.S.C. § 7701 et seq., https://www.law.cornell.edu/uscode/text/15/chapter-103
- FTC's CAN-SPAM Rule, 16 C.F.R. pt. 316, https://www.ftc.gov/enforcement/rules/rulemaking-regulatory-reform-proceedings/can-spam-rule
- Canada's Anti-Spam Legislation (CASL), http://fightspam.gc.ca/eic/site/030.nsf/eng/h_00211.html
- Canada's Electronic Commerce Protection Regulations (CRTC 2012-183), https://crtc.gc.ca/eng/archive/2012/2012-183.htm

- European Union's General Data Protection Regulation (Regulation (EU) 2016/679), https://eur-lex.europa.eu/eli/reg/2016/679/oj
- California's Anti-Spam Law (2004), Cal. Bus. & Prof. Code § 17529.5 https://leginfo.legislature.ca.gov/faces/codes_displaySection.xhtml?lawCode=BPC&sectionNum=17529.5
- California Consumer Privacy Act of 2018, Cal. Bus. & Prof. Code § 1798.100 et seq., https://leginfo.legislature.ca.gov/faces/billTextClient.xhtml?bill_id=201720180AB375

Disclosures And Disclaimers

This guide is published in print format. Neither the Author nor the Publisher makes any claim to the intellectual property rights of third party vendors, their subsidiaries, or related entities.

All trademarks and service marks are the properties of their respective owners. All references to these properties are made solely for editorial purposes. Except for marks actually owned by the Author or the Publisher, no commercial claims are made to their use, and neither the Author nor the Publisher is affiliated with such marks in any way.

Unless otherwise expressly noted, none of the individuals or business entities mentioned herein has endorsed the contents of this guide.

Limits of Liability & Disclaimers of Warranties

Because this guide is a general educational information product, it is not a substitute for professional advice on the topics discussed in it.

The materials in this guide are provided "as is" and without warranties of any kind either express or implied. The Author and the Publisher disclaim all warranties, express or implied, including, but not limited to, implied warranties of merchantability and fitness for a particular purpose. The Author and the Publisher do not warrant that defects will be corrected, or that any website or any server that makes this guide available is free of viruses or other harmful components. The Author does not warrant or make any representations regarding the use or the results of the use of the materials in this guide in terms of their correctness, accuracy, reliability, or otherwise. Applicable law may not allow the exclusion of implied warranties, so the above exclusion may not apply to you.

Under no circumstances, including, but not limited to, negligence, shall the Author or the Publisher be liable for any special or consequential damages that result from the use of, or the inability to use this guide, even if the Author, the Publisher, or an authorized representative has been advised of the possibility of such damages.

Applicable law may not allow the limitation or exclusion of liability or incidental or consequential damages, so the above limitation or exclusion may not apply to you. In no event shall the Author's or Publisher's total liability to you for all damages, losses, and causes of action (whether in contract, tort, including but not limited to, negligence or otherwise) exceed the amount paid by you, if any, for this guide.

You agree to hold the Author and the Publisher of this guide, principals, agents, affiliates, and employees harmless from any and all liability for all claims for damages due to injuries, including attorney fees and costs, incurred by you or caused to third parties by you, arising out of the products, services, and activities discussed in this guide, excepting only claims for gross negligence or intentional tort.

You agree that any and all claims for gross negligence or intentional tort shall be settled solely by confidential binding arbitration per the American Arbitration Association's commercial arbitration rules. All arbitration must occur in the municipality where the Author's principal place of business is located. Your claim cannot be aggregated with third party claims. Arbitration fees and costs shall be split equally, and you are solely responsible for your own lawyer fees.

Facts and information are believed to be accurate at the time they were placed in this guide. All data provided in this guide is to be used for information purposes only. The information contained within is not intended to provide specific legal, financial, tax, physical or mental health advice, or any other advice whatsoever, for any individual or company and should not be relied upon in that regard. The services described are only offered in jurisdictions where they may be legally offered. Information provided is not all-inclusive, and is limited to information that is made available and such information should not be relied upon as all-inclusive or accurate.

For more information about this policy, please contact the Author at the e-mail address listed in the Copyright Notice at the front of this guide.
IF YOU DO NOT AGREE WITH THESE TERMS AND EXPRESS CONDITIONS, DO NOT READ THIS GUIDE. YOUR USE OF THIS GUIDE, PRODUCTS, SERVICES, AND ANY PARTICIPATION IN ACTIVITIES MENTIONED IN THIS GUIDE, MEAN THAT YOU ARE AGREEING TO BE LEGALLY BOUND BY THESE TERMS.

Affiliate Compensation & Material Connections Disclosure

This guide may contain hyperlinks to websites and information created and maintained by other individuals and organizations. The Author and the Publisher do not control or guarantee the accuracy, completeness, relevance, or timeliness of any information or privacy policies posted on these linked websites.

You should assume that all references to products and services in this guide are made because material connections exist between the Author or Publisher and the providers of the mentioned products and services ("Provider").

You should also assume that all hyperlinks within this guide are affiliate links for (a) the Author, (b) the Publisher, or (c) someone else who is an affiliate for the mentioned products and services (individually and collectively, the "Affiliate").

The Affiliate recommends products and services in this guide based in part on a good faith belief that the purchase of such products or services will help readers in general.

The Affiliate has this good faith belief because (a) the Affiliate has tried the product or service mentioned prior to recommending it or (b) the Affiliate has researched the reputation of the Provider and has made the decision to recommend the Provider's products or services based on the Provider's history of providing these or other products or services.

The representations made by the Affiliate about products and services reflect the Affiliate's honest opinion based upon the facts known to the Affiliate at the time this guide was published.

Because there is a material connection between the Affiliate and Providers of products or services mentioned in this guide, you should always assume that the Affiliate may be biased because of the Affiliate's relationship with a Provider and/or because the Affiliate has received or will receive something of value from a Provider.

Perform your own due diligence before purchasing a product or service mentioned in this guide.

The type of compensation received by the Affiliate may vary. In some instances, the Affiliate may receive complimentary products (such as a review copy), services, or money from a Provider prior to mentioning the Provider's products or services in this guide.

In addition, the Affiliate may receive a monetary commission or non-monetary compensation when you take action by clicking on a hyperlink in this guide. This includes, but is not limited to, when you purchase a product or service from a Provider after clicking on an affiliate link in this guide.

Purchase Price

Although the Publisher believes the price is fair for the value that you receive, you understand and agree that the purchase price for this guide has been arbitrarily set by the Publisher or the vendor who sold you this guide. This price bears no relationship to objective standards.

Due Diligence

You are advised to do your own due diligence when it comes to making any decisions. Use caution and seek the advice of qualified professionals before acting upon the contents of this guide or any other information. You shall not consider any examples, documents, or other content in this guide or otherwise provided by the Author or Publisher to be the equivalent of professional advice.

The Author and the Publisher assume no responsibility for any losses or damages resulting from your use of any link, information, or opportunity contained in this guide or within any other information disclosed by the Author or the Publisher in any form whatsoever.

YOU SHOULD ALWAYS CONDUCT YOUR OWN INVESTIGATION (PERFORM DUE DILIGENCE) BEFORE BUYING PRODUCTS OR SERVICES FROM ANYONE OFFLINE OR VIA THE INTERNET. THIS INCLUDES PRODUCTS AND SERVICES SOLD VIA HYPERLINKS CONTAINED IN THIS GUIDE.

Made in United States
Orlando, FL
08 January 2024